The Mother's Day Gift

By

Patricia Dunfey Hoyt

Dragonfly Publishing

Thornton, NH

First Edition

Dedication

To: Barbara, our mother, Mimi
We Love You More!
P.D.H.

To:
Marisol, my constant inspiration
B.B.

ISBN: 978-1-7378-6864-4 [Hard Cover]
ISBN: 978-1-7378-6865-1 [Paperback]
ISBN: 978-1-7378-6863-7 [E-Book]
Library of Congress Catalog # [PENDING]

Illustrations on the front cover and throughout the book
created by Bill Batson
Cover and book design: Beverly A. Hodsdon, Joyce Design Solutions LLC.

Foreward

For your loved ones,

Always, Look for the signs!

Table of Contents

Dedication   i

Foreward   ii

Table of Contents   iii

Introduction:
Mother's Day Weekend   7

Chapter 1:   Sailing Lessons   15

Chapter 2: Yachting   25

Chapter 3: Gardening   29

Chapter 4: Hiking   35

Chapter 5: The Classroom   43

Chapter 6: Celebration of Life   49

Chapter 7: A Walk in the Woods   65

After Mention   69

About the Author   72

About the Illustrator   73

Introduction:
Mother's Day Weekend

It was Sunday, Mother's Day, and my mother had a gift she wanted to give to me. So I drove to her home for a visit.

It was springtime in New England, and I arrived at my mother's home. The sun was shining, the wind was blowing, and the last piles of snow on the pavement were melting from April's surprise snow storm.

Soon the grass would turn green, the buds on the tree branches would unravel to reveal leaves, and the sun would shine and feel warm upon our skin.

My mother and I sat in the living room looking out the window at the tree branches blowing. We sat and talked about summer.

We dreamt, anticipating warmer weather. Looking forward to sailing in Maine on my sister-in-law Kim and my brother Sean's sailboat.

School for me would be over in a month's time, and I would have more time to spend with my mother doing things she enjoyed.

My mother said to me, "I got you a little gift for Mother's Day. Here it is! Open it!"

The small package was wrapped in white paper with a pink ribbon and a bow. As I unwrapped the package, I noticed a transparent box with an artistic, colorful dragonfly inside. It was made out of wire and plastic, and had a suction cup, so that it could be attached to a window.

Inside the clear box there was also a little note about the dragonfly.

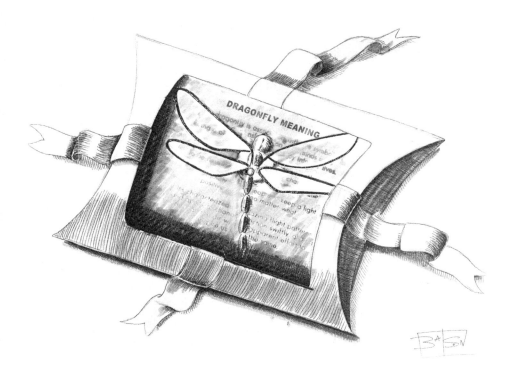

"On the note was a story about the dragon-fly symbolizing transformation." My mother said, "It reminds me of a stained glass dragonfly. Like the kind Les's sister, Pam, makes. I thought you would like it, and you could stick it to your window at home as a suncatcher."

"Thanks mom! I will! I will put it on the window when I get home," I said.

Time; if only I knew, time was slipping away for my mother.

When I got home later that day, I stuck the dragonfly to my window. The sunlight shining on the dragonfly made it shimmer and look real.

I didn't know it at the time, but this would be the last gift I would receive from my mother.

CHAPTER 1
Sailing

It is June, and school is out!

Warmer days are finally here!

Time to play and have fun! "Whee! I am free! It is summertime," I think to myself.

It's Monday, sailing day. I am sailing with the wind in my face and my hair blowing behind me in the breeze. I am learning how to sail on Lake Winnipesaukee.

My friend Edna and I are taking sailing lessons together. We learn sailing terms such as how to tack and how to jibe. We learn the parts of a boat, how a sail works, and basic sailing instructions. We take turns at the tiller, steering the sailboat, and saying the commands.

Edna says, "Prepare to tack."

In order to sail a sailboat you need to make a zig zag plan to cross the water to get to a given point. Sailboats can not sail straight into the wind. This area is called the NO GO ZONE. When a sailboat goes from a zig to a zag this is called a tack. To tack is to turn the bow (the front of the boat) through the wind from one side of the NO GO ZONE to the other.

During a tack, the sails of the sailboat also cross to the other side of the boat. It is important when sailing to talk to the crew, this is done for safety reasons.

Helmsman Edna checks for anything that could be in the way of where she wants to tack to. She selects a point to where she wants to steer toward. Then calls out, "Ready about!"

I check to see if the jib sheet is clear and ready to run out. I uncleat and hold the working jib sheet, getting ready to sheet in the lazy jib sheet before saying, "Ready!"

Then, the helmsman calls out, "Tacking!" She does this to tell me that she is beginning to tack and turn the boat through the wind.

The boat turns into the wind and the sail begins to luff. I release the working jib so the jib can cross over to the other side of the boat.

We cross over to the other side of the boat but something is wrong, there is no wind. We are in the NO GO ZONE! The sails have lost their power!

We tacked the boat too slowly and got stuck in the NO GO ZONE. We are now in a term called irons. The sails are luffing. The boat comes to a stop! The rudder no longer steers the boat. We are not moving! We check to see which way the wind is blowing, and we make adjustments.

When all of a sudden...

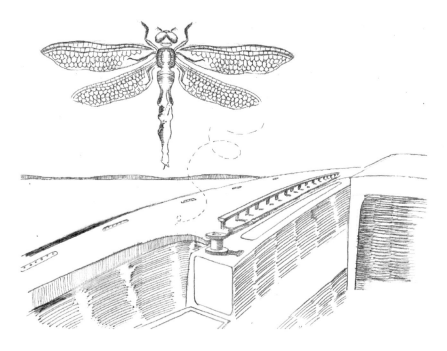

...a dragonfly lands on the port, or left, side of the cabin trunk of the sailboat. It lingers, enjoying the ride.

Dragonflies are interesting insects. They live by water and have two big eyes that touch each other. They have two pairs of strong transparent wings. Each wing has patterns on it. The dragonfly has an elongated body that is black.

It is able to fly by maneuvering quickly, swiftly and quietly at a moment's notice.

The dragonfly studies me and seems to enjoy sailing as much as my mother did!

It rotates its body, then flies away.

The sailboat sits in the water waiting for wind. We drift, waiting for the wind to pick up. Lucky for us it does, and we return to the lake shore to anchor the sailboat.

Chapter 2
Yachting

On Tuesday, my friend Les and I met up with Pam and Captain Bob. They invited us out on their Regal Commodore 3860 40 foot yacht on Lake Winnipesaukee. It is a sunny and breezy day. I am sunning myself as I lay stretched out on the stern, which is the back of the boat. I am enjoying cruising on the yacht in the warm sunshine. I am happy to have a mindless day of just enjoying being alive and free with no cares in the world.

As I sit enjoying myself, I think of my mother, and how if she was here, how she would love to feel the sunshine upon her skin and the wind blowing her hair. She loved going out on Pam and Robert's Yacht.

When all of a sudden...

...a dragonfly lands on my leg!

It studies me, and I study it.

The dragonfly seems to be enjoying the sunshine as much as I am. It has two big eyes and a long exoskeleton body. It has a head, a thorax, an abdomen, and six legs.

It has color patches on its four wings. This dragonfly resembles the dragonfly gift my mother gave me that is on my window at home.

The dragonfly gracefully turns and flies away.

CHAPTER 3
Gardening

It's Wednesday, gardening day! Time to get the soil ready for planting. Les uses the rototiller to turn the soil and prepare the soil for planting. Then, he uses a hoe to mound the soil into long piles that look like logs. Next, he tips the hoe using the edge to make a groove in the soil. The groove is where we will place the seeds.

The seed package instructions tell us how deep to make the groove, since each type of seed needs a different depth.

I plant the seeds using the seeder. As I walk slowly down the row, with the seeder in my hand I release the seeds, putting the new seed a couple inches away from the last one. After I sow the seeds, Les uses the hoe to cover the seeds with the right amount of dirt which it states on the package.

We continue in this fashion until all the rows have been planted. Then, we water all the rows.

This year we planted brussel sprouts, swiss chard, kale, lettuce, beets, carrots, green beans, and arugula. As well as, summer squash, zucchini and tomatoes.

As I finish watering the rows, all of a sudden...

..a dragonfly darts right at me!

I don't have time to duck or get out of its way! I feel the air blow in my face, as the dragonfly swerves and flies off!

"That dragonfly almost hit me!", I say to Les.

It's a good thing that dragonflies are expert fliers with the ability to maneuver quickly, because I would not have been able to get out of its way!

That would have hurt if the dragonfly flew into me, I say to myself.

Chapter 4
Hiking

On Thursday, my brother Peter, his wife Theo and my friend Sue and I go hiking. We all pack backpacks with the necessary essentials for hiking in the White Mountains of New Hampshire.

In my pack, I include two 16 ounce bottles of water, some G.O.R.P. (Good Old Raisins & Peanuts), lunch which consists of a peanut butter and jelly sandwich, two tangerines, a few walnuts and a piece of mozzarella string cheese. I also include a map, a compass, matches and paper, a tarp, a first aid kit, a waterproof rain jacket and a lightweight down jacket, a headlamp, gloves and a hat.

Our packs are about 30-35 pounds as we climb up Mt. Avolon, Mt. Tom and Mt. Field. Mt. Tom and Mt. Field peaks are over 4,000 feet, they are part of the group of mountains known as the 48 4,000 footers.

Peter tells me that, " When you climb more than one mountain, it is called 'peak bagging'."

We climb up and up and up the mountain which is called ascending, until we reach the top, the summit. The journey is slow but we finally reach Mt. Avalon's summit, and the views are breathtaking. We see a sea of mountains that go on forever. It is so peaceful and beautiful and welcoming. This soothes my soul and I feel healing starting to take hold.

Next, we climb Mt. Tom and then Mt. Field. It feels so good to breathe in the mountain air, and feel the warm sunshine on my face and skin. We take our lunch out of our backpacks on the summit to have a picnic. I am thrilled to be hiking with family members and a friend who enjoys hiking as much as I do!

After lunch, we decide to head down the mountain and not to bag another peak. There is another mountain called Mt. Willey that we would do too, if we had time. We base our decision on how long it took us to get up the mountain and how far we would have to travel to get to the next peak and then down the mountain again. We want to be in the parking lot before the sun goes down because we do not want to hike in the dark. So we head down the trail, which is called descending. We follow the trail blazes, which are painted lines on rocks and trees that mark the trail back to the parking lot.

At the base of the mountain there is a railroad depot near the parking lot where we decide to stop to rest our legs. We all sit down on the steps to relax after the long hike.

We take off our shoes and socks which feels great on our sore feet. As I stand on the railroad station porch to stretch my legs, all of a sudden...

...a dragonfly appears out of nowhere!

It flies around the corner of the railroad depot and heads right for me! Turning abruptly a split second before it almost hits my face. The dragonfly twists and turns its body avoiding a collision with me! I am thankful once again for this near miss.

I am so surprised to see another dragonfly!

"This is so crazy," I thought to myself, " I have seen so many dragonfly encounters this summer!"

CHAPTER 5
The Classroom

It is Friday, and I am at school packing away boxes to use with my students next year. I am organizing my room before it is professionally cleaned by the custodial staff, who work at our school during the summer months.

As I am organizing materials, all of a sudden...

.....a dragonfly flies into my classroom!

I am stunned. "Wow, no way!

Another dragonfly? I can't believe it!"

I have seen so many dragonflies this summer!

I have never seen any in my life before this!

"What is going on?" I think to myself.

I decide to do something quick so the dragonfly doesn't get lost in the building, and unable to find its way out.

As I am thinking, the dragonfly hovers above me like a helicopter. Then, it turns and flies to the closed windows, where it bounces numerous times off of the windowpane.

Grabbing a butterfly net from the science corner of my classroom, I approach the dragonfly. I swoop the net to the right, and miss. I swoop to the left, and miss.

I try to catch it with the net, but dragonflies are masters of flight and speed. I try again and again and miss!

I think out loud and say, "Mom, is that you?

Please let me catch you or you will not be able to find your way out of the building."

Swishing the net in the air, I finally catch the dragonfly with the net up against the windowpane.

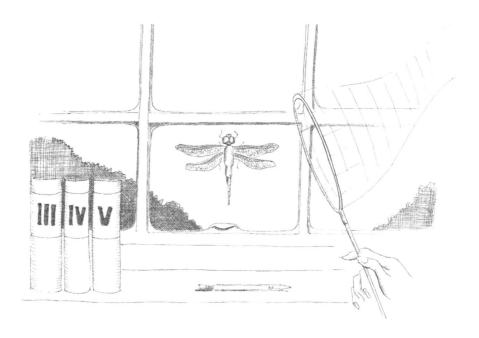

I carefully cover the opening of the net with my free hand, as I quickly walk down the hall and out the side entrance to the school.

"I am so happy I caught the dragonfly." Once outside, I remove my hand and release the dragonfly from the net.

As it flies away...

... I say, "Good-bye Mom!"

I am so relieved to have caught her and so happy to set her free!

Chapter 6
Celebration of Life

On Saturday, my siblings and I held a funeral mass, ceremonial burial, and a celebration of life gathering for our mother who passed away in May from complications due to colon cancer.

The funeral mass for our mother was held in Bedford, N.H. My brother's Peter and Sean, and my son Gordon were the pallbearers. Close friends and family members spoke in remembrance of our mother to the congregation. The funeral mass was beautiful with organ music, a soloist, and prayers. I know our mother would have loved it and was smiling down from heaven.

After the mass, we traveled north to the cemetery.

At the burial, My friend read a reflection that I wrote about my mother.

My Mother

I have been very fortunate to have my mother in my life for many years.

During the course of my life I have enjoyed being in my mother's company. My mother and I loved singing songs and dancing. At age thirteen, I was down at the Rustic Nail Lounge with my mother and our dear friend Floretta, when a man asked me to dance. I didn't know how to dance, but my mother and Flo said, "Just move your body to the music." So I did, and have been dancing ever since.

I loved going on errands with my mother. I would ask if she was going to go to The Cheese Shop in Concord Center and if she said yes then, I would go with her. At The Cheese Shop, they let you taste and sample each cheese before you would buy it. My mother loved tasting different kinds of cheese and I loved learning about the cheese and eating it too!

During the course of my life, my mother has seen me at my worst and best. She has given a lot of advice to me about fashion, hair cuts, style, and how to raise my children. Sometimes I listened to her advice, and sometimes I ignored it.

My mother has been involved in her children's lives as well as her grand-children's. She is very proud of our accomplishments. She was present at our birthdays, sport games, theater events, fun excursions, graduations and holiday gatherings. She joined us on whole family trips to Florida, Ireland and Israel.

These last few years, I have enjoyed our time together. Going out to eat at her favorite restaurants, The Bedford Village Inn, The Grand, The Puritan and T-Bones. It has been fun shopping with my mother at Smitten's Boutique, Marshalls and HomeGoods.

For the past several years, my siblings and I have watched my mother fight cancer with strength, determination, and courage!

I am very thankful that we got to spend a lot of time together, to visit and talk about family stories and the hereafter.

As time went on and the medicine took its toll. We no longer went out to restaurants or shopping. It was our turn to give back to her. My sister Catherine, and I would take turns caring for our mother. When it was our turn we would buy her food, take her shopping, cook her meals, clean up, and make her bed.

I would sit and talk about life and death with my mother. We talked about God and what each of us believed about heaven. My mother and I both believe in God and that we will spiritually see each other again in the afterlife.

"It is said that when you believe, signs turn up everywhere."

This I believe to be true, because this past spring and summer, signs started appearing everywhere.

Two weeks before my mother died she gave me a dragonfly suncatcher gift that looked like a stained glass dragonfly.

During the spring and summertime, I had five dragonfly encounters!

Or should I say my mother arrived as an angel on dragonfly wings.

She was coming to me to show me she was transformed.

I found these encounters to be very unusual since I had never seen dragonflies before.

I do not doubt that these encounters were signs of the afterlife and my mother had been transformed into a dragonfly.

She had been sending me the dragonflies to let me know she was ok and that I needed to be reminded of her presence.

A message for me. She had transformed to another realm.

"It is said in the Native American culture that dragonflies are the embodiment of spirits that have already gone on. They are the bringers of dreams from the afterlife."

"The Japanese believe that dragonflies are symbolic of success, victory, happiness, strength and courage. Dragonflies urge you to look beyond illusions and see the truth that is right in front of you."

"Dragonflies signify a path to new worlds. They are about transformation and a change in perspective, energy, potential, and maturity, depth of character, power and poise. The dragonfly navigates with elegance and grace."

Now, doesn't that sound like what my mother would transform into!

At the burial, a nice size group of family and friends gathers at the gravesite. The granite gravestone is engraved with my mother's name, birth and death date. The beautiful handcrafted dovetailed wooden box that my brother Sean made, rests on top of the grave. I think our mother would have been so proud to have seen it, and honored to be encased in it. An assortment of pretty flowers from her sisters, Nancy and Winnie embellishes the box and gravesite.

We gather in a large circle holding hands, while my former husband and good friend Tom sings *"In The Garden,"* by C. Austin Miles which was one of my mother's favorite songs.

He also sings *"Will The Circle Be Unbroken,"* by Ada R. Habershon (the Carter Family, The Nitty, Gritty, Dirt Band). Tom has a beautiful voice and has been singing since he was young. He sings from the heart and everyone is moved by his voice and singing.

I start crying and crying. It is the perfect, and most beautiful farewell for our mother.

I am happy and sad at the same time. Sad to say good-bye to my mother, but happy to celebrate her life with all her friends and family. I am so pleased at the beauty of the gathering at the gravesite with all of us connected and holding hands. It touches my soul, my inner core, and reminds me of my mother's last words to me,

"Death is a continuation of life."

And so it is!

After the burial ceremony, my siblings and I have a party called a *'Celebration of Life'* to honor our mother and her life.

Family members and friends come by my house to celebrate our mother's life and share memories.

We serve food and refreshments to everyone.

At the celebration my daughter Tatyana shows a video made of pictures taken throughout her Mimi's (grandmother's) life. The video is set to some of Mimi's favorite music. There is a great turn out of friends and family who come to our mother's party.

As I stand in the driveway by the garage, saying good-bye to my mother's good friend Betty, all of a sudden...

...a dragonfly comes up the driveway.

The dragonfly circles around Betty and I. It flies around us twice before flying over to Betty's car. Where the dragonfly circles the car once, before turning and flying away. Betty and I turn to look at each other, and at the same time say...

... "She's here!"

CHAPTER 7
Walking in the Woods

On Sunday, Peter, Theo, Les and I decide to go for a walk in the woods to Rainbow Falls on the Walter/Newton Natural Area Trail. We pull into the parking lot and park our cars.

As we get ready to start the hike, all of a sudden...

...Les says, "Look there's a dragonfly!"

It glides through the air, hovering here and there before flying away. I think to myself, "That's it, there she goes. We won't see her anymore." I am sad thinking this is the last time I will see her.

We start our walk on the Walter/Newton Trail following the blazes on the trees that lead to our destination.

We arrive at Rainbow Falls, and see a huge boulder with a waterfall cascading down it to a clear brook below. We take pictures of this beautiful site before heading back down the trail.

As we approach the parking lot, all of a sudden...

...my brother Peter says, "There's a dragonfly by our car!"

Sure enough, there is!

The dragonfly darts, twisting and turning as if waving good-bye as it flies over and around my brother's car.

"There she is!," My brother says.

"Yes, it is her!

Our mother!," I say.

The End

After Mention

This story of many encounters with a

dragonfly did occur in the summer of 2019

in the year my mother died. The incidents

happened from June until September,

when my mother was laid to rest.

Who would have ever thought that a

Mother's Day Gift of a Dragonfly Suncatcher

could mean so much to me, and help heal

the heartache and loss of losing our mother.

This is the note that was inside the gift that I received with the dragonfly from my mother.

"The Dragonfly Meaning Statement"

Quote from www.loftfifty5.com

"The Dragonfly Meaning ... The dragonfly is associated with the symbolic meaning of transformation. It reminds us to bring a bit more lightness and joy into our lives.

When the spirit animal shows up, it's an indication that it is time for change. To be flexible and adaptable in any situation.

The dragonfly invites people to keep a light positive outlook no matter what.

It's characterized by amazing flight

patterns and ability to change directions swiftly, gliding through the air with no apparent effort to inspire us to do the same.

When you have brave wings ... you fly!!"

*We Helen & Diane, owners of Loft Fifty 5 give special permission to Patricia Hoyt to use our **"Dragonfly Meaning Statement"** for the use in her book **"The Mother's Day Gift"** by Patricia Dunfey Hoyt. This statement can be used only for this project for copies in her books. Permission was granted on March 30, 2021.*

About the Author

Hi, I am Patricia Dunfey Hoyt. I was a teacher for thirty-four years and retired from that profession in 2020.

I have two adult children Tatyana and Gordon, and I live in Thornton, NH. with my partner Lester. I have a cat named Smokey and a grand-dog named Benji.

©Jane Lapriore

I have purchased a wrought iron bench with wooden slats to sit upon and look out over our garden. We have planted some Black-Eyed Susan's to honor my mother and attract dragonflies to our yard.

We also have a bird bath because dragonflies love water.

Did you know that dragonflies eat up to 100 mosquitos a day? Now, isn't that a great reason to have a dragonfly in your yard!

I hope you enjoyed my special true story called, **The Mother's Day Gift!**

About the Illustrator

Bill Batson is a writer, artist and activist. He has published a sketch and short essay book called, **Nyack Sketch Log** every week since 2011. Bill is the manager and artist in residence at the Nyack Farmers Market and an advisor to River Hook: the Hester Haring Cason Preserve in Upper Nyack, N.Y. In June 2021, Bill was inducted into the Rockland County Hall Civil Rights Hall of Fame.

©Orpheus Acosta

Made in the USA
Monee, IL
11 April 2023

31074776R00044